My Mommy's on a Business Trip

by Phaedra Cucina
illustrated by Shelley Johannes

DolceVita Press, LLC

Order a customized version

Order a customized version of **My Mommy's on a Business Trip** for employee or customer gifts and create a unique, lasting connection to your brand and company. For example, books can be customized to include a letter from your CEO recognizing and thanking employees for the sacrifices they make while traveling for work.

Contact Special Sales at info@dolcevitawoman.com for more information.

ISBN: 978-0-9818807-09

First Edition: October, 2008

Illustrations and Book Design by Shelley Johannes
Maps designed by Chris Erichsen

Printed in Canada

Special Thanks

This book would not be here today if not for the support and love of my dear husband, Carlo, and my parents, who taught me to believe I can achieve anything I want to. Shelley Johannes' vision and talent brought this book to life and I will be forever grateful to have found such a wonderful partner. I will always hold in my heart the amazing women who believed in the birth of this book - Deb Bauer, Sandra Bucklin, Kathryn Davis, Tonja Eaton, Holly Edger, Claudia Esquivel, Ellen Fenwick, Karen Fuller, Liz Howard, Anna Kuhn, Xenia Maradiaga, Fiona McInally, and Carlene Wegmann Todd. I would also like to thank the mamas who graciously agreed to review and endorse the first drafts of the book – Maria Bailey, June Blocklin, Lynn Cranford, Shawn Dennis, Jen Dorre, Lee Harper, Becky Higgins, Joyce Mullen, Linda Rebrovick, and Kya Sainsbury-Carter. Finally, a special nod to Lavelle Carlson, my publishing mentor, and to Scott Prath, for introducing the two of us.

For Chloe and Max

My inspiration, my joy, my sun and moon.
I love you both so much it melts my heart, everyday.

Join us at www.dolcevitawoman.com and tell us how you and your family
handle business trips, share tips with successful road warrior moms, and
discuss other issues facing busy, professional women.

We want to hear your point of view!

Where do you go most often on business trips?
Let us know at www.dolcevitawoman.com, and you could help create
the next book in the My Mommy's on a Business Trip series.

My Mommy's on a business trip.

She gave me
a big hug and kiss
before she left,

and she calls me
at night,

but
I miss her
very much!

I think she's having
lots of fun,

riding on trains

and
flying
in planes...

...and even
going around
in those
**big yellow
cars.**

I'm sure her hotel has a

great **big** swimming pool
she can **play** in, too!

She'll talk to her friends
at **lunch**

and have a super-fun time.

My Mommy had to go away
because **her work**
helps our family

and **makes her happy.**

Every night,
when she's back in
her hotel room

-- after
her dinner
and her bath --

she calls
to tell me
she loves me
and ask me what
I did today.

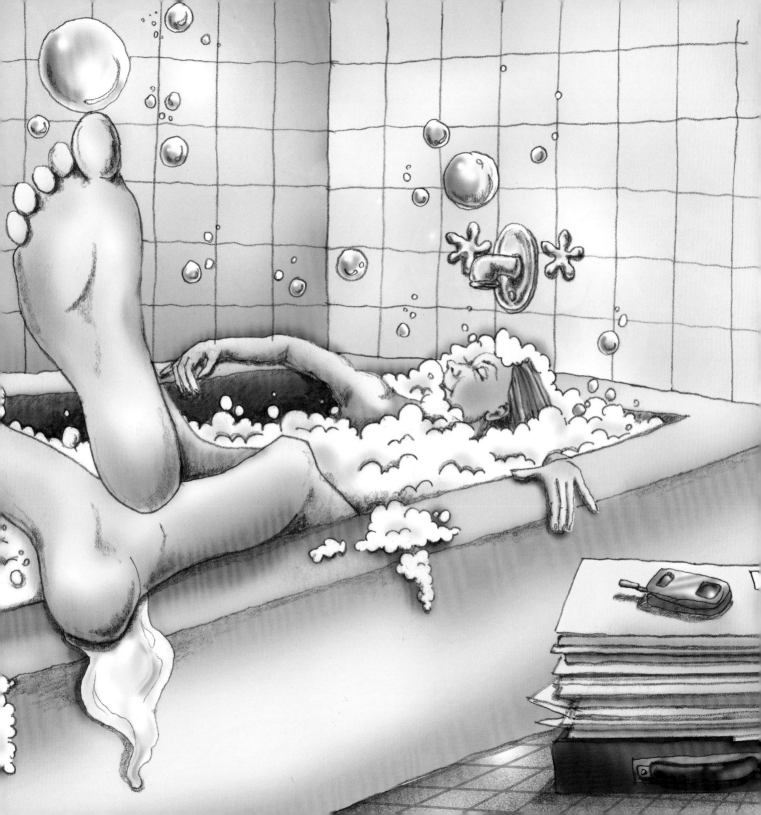

I'm **happy** to hear her voice,
but I also feel a little sad. I remember that she's far away.
But my Mommy tells me every night
that she's coming back.

She **always** comes back!

My Mommy's
on a
business
trip...

but she misses me and
**she's coming home
real soon!**

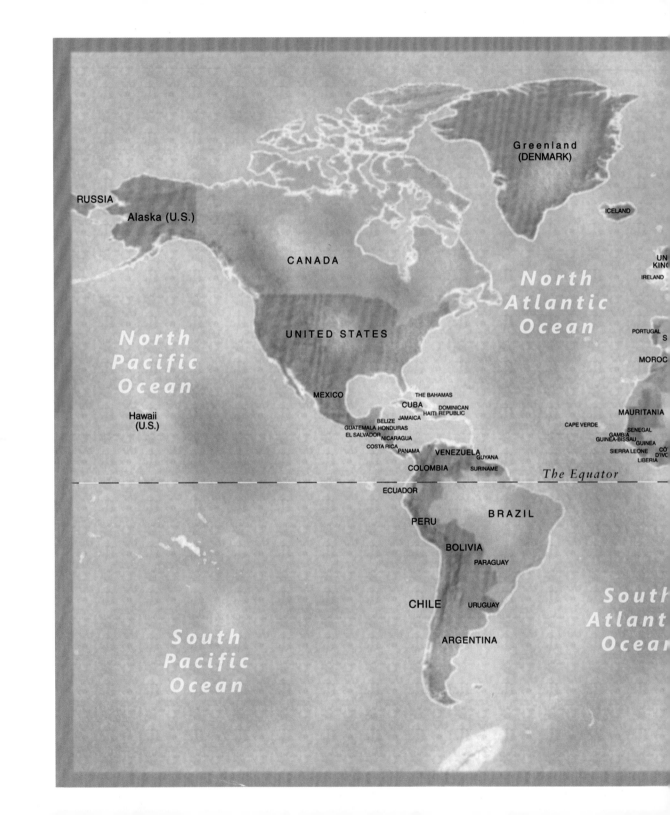

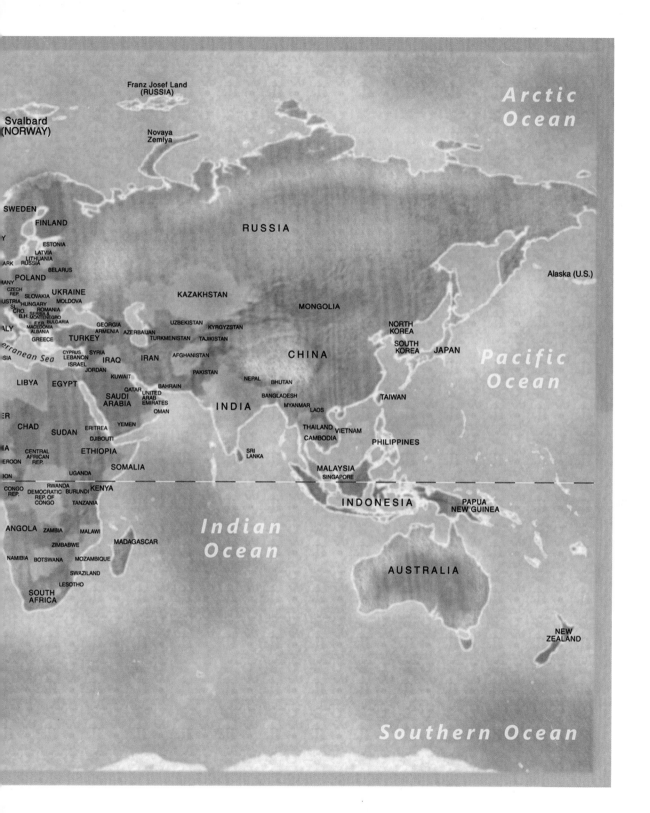

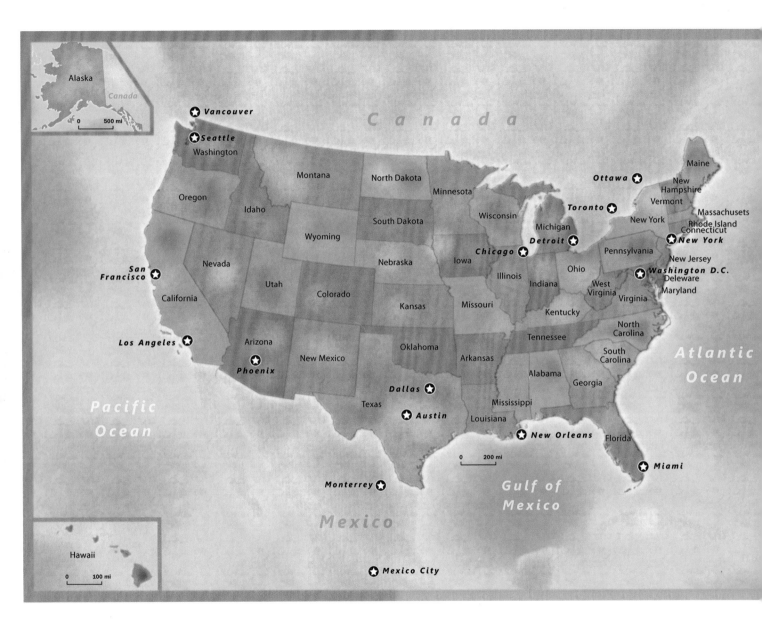